NEW WAY

EASY START

Sp

Written by aines

Illustrated by Nina O'Connell

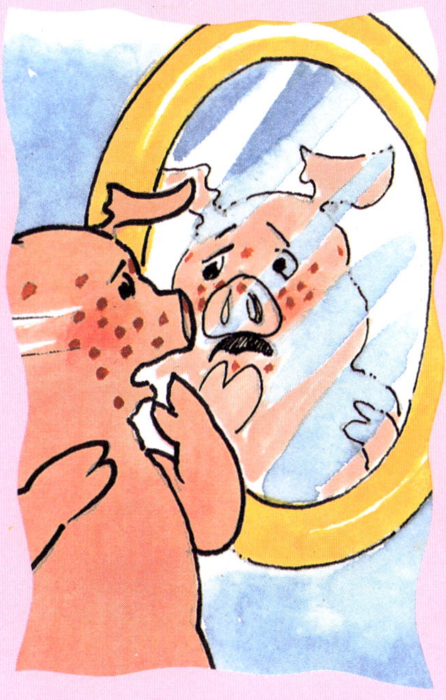

Nelson

"You have a spot,"
said Meg the hen.

"You have a spot,"
said Deb the rat.

“You have a spot,”
said Ben the dog.

"1 2 3 4 5 6,"

said Meg the hen.

"You have six spots."

"I have six spots,"

said Pat the pig.

“No,”

said Deb the rat.

“You don’t have six spots.”

“You have lots of spots.
Lots and lots of spots.
You are ill.”

“Go to bed,”

said Ben.

“Go to bed,”

said Meg.

Pat the pig sat in bed.

Lots of spots.

Pat the pig sat in bed.

Big spots.

Pat the pig sat in bed.

Little spots.

No spots.

"No spots,"

said Pat the pig.

"I can go to school."

“I can’t see Meg the hen.

I can’t see Deb the rat.

I can’t see Ben the dog.

"They are not in school,"
said Sam.

"They have spots,"
said Jip.